Case Studies
in Operational Culture

Paula Holmes-Eber, PhD

Major Marcus J. Mainz

MARINE CORPS UNIVERSITY PRESS
QUANTICO, VIRGINIA
2014

This book would not have been made possible without the generous assistance and support of the Marine Corps University, School of Advanced Warfighting (SAW). We would like to thank SAW's director, Colonel Michael F. Morris, and the graduates of the SAW class of 2013 for their willingness to pass on their operational culture lessons of the past decade.

We are also deeply indebted to the tireless editorial assistance of Andrea Hamlen and Stase Rodebaugh at the Marine Corps University Leadership Communication Skills Center.

Table of Contents

Joint Operations

List of Contributors

Lieutenant Colonel Justin J. Ansel Jr. graduated from Louisiana State University and received his commission in December 1995. Colonel Ansel's operational tours included: platoon commander and company executive officer for 1st Battalion, 1st Marines; future operations officer for 13th Marine Expeditionary Unit (Special Operations Capable); platoon commander for Marine Barracks, Guantanamo Bay, Cuba; team leader, Georgia Train and Equip Program; company commander for 3d Battalion, 6th Marines; military advisor, 22d Naval Construction Regiment; and executive officer for 1st Battalion, 8th Marines. Ansel participated in two Western Pacific deployments with the 13th MEU (SOC), Operation Enduring Freedom (OEF), and Operation Iraqi Freedom (OIF). He is currently serving as the MAGTF plans officer for U.S. Marine Corps Forces, South. Colonel Ansel is a graduate of the Marine Corps Expeditionary Warfare School, Command and Staff College, and the School of Advanced Warfighting. He is married to the former Laura Ward. They have five dogs and a horse.

Lieutenant Colonel David K. Aragon graduated from North Dakota State University with a degree in aeronautical engineering and manufacturing and was commissioned in the U.S. Air Force in 1998. From 2000 to 2007, he held a variety of B-52 assignments, including serving as the instructor radar navigator and wing weapons officer. In May 2008, Colonel Aragon became the first U.S. Air Force aviator to fulfill a request for forces (RFF) billet for a joint task force and reported to Hurlburt Field, Florida, to undergo Pilatus U-28A qualification. In 2010, he was selected for duty as the first Air Force Global Strike Command liaison officer to Air Combat Command-Weapons and Tactics, Langley Air Force Base, Virginia. Aragon has deployed in support of OEF and OIF, where he flew more than 130 combat sorties and 1,000 combat hours in both the B-52H and U-28A. His decorations include the Air Force Meritorious Service Medal with one oak leaf; the Air Medal with six oak leaf clusters; and the Aerial Achievement Medal. He is a graduate of the Air Command and Staff College at Maxwell Air Force Base, Alabama, and the Marine Corps School of Advanced Warfighting. He is now assigned to Combined Forces Command, United States Forces-Korea, as an operational level joint planner.

Major Carrie C. Batson graduated from Pepperdine University with a degree in history. After receiving her commission, Major Batson became a public affairs officer (PAO) and was assigned to the 1st Marine Division. She then served as the PAO for the 11th Marine Expeditionary Unit, where she conducted one deployment in support of OEF (Horn of Africa) and humanitarian efforts in East Timor, and two combat tours in Iraq supporting OIF. She then became the PAO for Marine Corps Installations West and led the Consolidated Public Affairs Office aboard Camp Pendleton, California. Upon assignment to Headquarters Marine Corps, she served as the advocate for public affairs capability development. She holds master's degrees in communication from San Diego State University and in both military studies and operational studies from Marine Corps University. Major Batson is currently deployed to International Security Assistance Force (ISAF) Headquarters in Kabul, Afghanistan.

Major Bradley P. Bean is a Marine air-ground task force (MAGTF) intelligence officer. Major Bean is a graduate of the Marine Corps Amphibious Warfare School and the School of Advanced Warfighting. He is currently the G-5 at U.S. Marine Forces-Korea (MARFORK).

Lieutenant Colonel Derek M. Brannon graduated from the Georgia Institute of Technology in 1996 with a bachelor's degree in industrial engineering. He has supported both Operations Noble Eagle and Iraqi Freedom as an F/A-18 pilot and forward air controller. Brannon served as the Marine Corps subject matter expert in NON-RF SAMS, surface-to-air threat countertactics, and the FA-18 electronic warfare suite while assigned to Marine Aviation Weapons and Tactics Squadron 1 (MAWTS-1). In June 2012, Colonel Brannon reported to the Marine Corps School of Advanced Warfighting and earned a master's degree in operational studies. Brannon is currently assigned as the Marine Corps Forces-Europe deliberate plans officer.

Major Jason A. Borovies is a career infantry officer who served as a rifle company commander and battalion operations officer during deployments to Iraq. He also served as the commanding officer of Recruiting Station Houston, Texas, and managed the acquisition of medical information technology programs while assigned to Marine Corps Systems Command. He is a 1998 graduate of The Citadel and a 2013 graduate of the Marine Corps School of Advanced Warfighting. Borovies is currently assigned as a plans officer with Marine Forces Central Command (Forward) in Bahrain.

Lieutenant Colonel Eric C. Dill was commissioned 14 December 1996. His assignments include tours with the Joint POW/MIA Accounting Command, Joint Special Operations Command, JTF-134 Detainee Operations, and two tours with 1st Marine Division, 1st Reconnaissance Battalion. He is a graduate of the Marine Corps Expeditionary Warfare School Distance Education Program, Command and Staff College, and the School of Advanced Warfighting. Colonel Dill is currently assigned as the Korea plans officer with III Marine Expeditionary Force.

Major Corey J. Frederickson graduated with a degree in applied military psychology from Royal Roads Military College and was commissioned as an officer in the Princess Patricia's Canadian Light Infantry in 1995. His career duties have included rifle platoon commander, mortar platoon commander, basic infantry officer instructor, rifle company commander, and staff officer at Army Headquarters. His operational tours have included Kosovo (KFOR) in 1999 as an area of operations commander, Afghanistan (OEF/ISAF) in 2006 as Battle Group S1, and ISAF again in 2008 as a Kandak Senior Mentor with the Operational Mentor and Liaison Team. Major Frederickson attended the Marine Corps Command and Staff College from 2011 to 2012 and the School of Advanced Warfighting from 2012 to 2013. After graduation, Frederickson returned to Canada and is currently employed as a staff planner for Strategic Joint Staff in Ottawa.

Major John C. Gianopoulos received his commission after graduating from Macalester College in 1998. As an infantry officer,

Gianopoulos has commanded at the platoon and company level and has served as an advisor to both an Iraqi Army battalion and an Afghanistan National Army battalion during combat operations. He has also served in several staff assignments as an infantry battalion executive officer, a training officer for the 2d Marine Logistics Group, FAST Company executive officer, and the officer in charge of the Marine Corps' Close Quarters Battle School. Major Gianopoulos is a graduate of the Marine Corps Expeditionary Warfare School, Command and Staff College, and School of Advanced Warfighting. His personal decorations include the Bronze Star Medal.

Major Brandon W. Graham was commissioned in the U.S. Marine Corps in 1997. He is an infantry officer and currently serves as the 1st Marine Division plans officer. Graham is married to the former Jolanda de Jong of the Netherlands. They live in San Clemente, California, with their two children, Justin (age 19) and Kaelyn (age 9).

Lieutenant Commander Adam (A. J.) Kruppa is a U.S. Navy surface warfare officer and currently is a joint force planner at U.S. European Command (US EUCOMHQ) J5 Plans. He has served aboard the USS *Nicholson* (DD 982), USS *Arthur W. Radford* (DD 968), USS *Firebolt* (PC 10), USS *Laboon* (DDG 58), and COMDESRON TWO EIGHT (CDS 28). He has completed tours as boarding officer, damage control assistant, operations officer, and executive officer. Kruppa completed master's degrees in both military and operational studies from Marine Corps University and is a graduate of the Command and Staff College, as well as the School of Advanced Warfighting. Kruppa currently serves on the board of directors for the Center for International Maritime Security (CIMSEC).

Major Steven Leutner is a strategist on the Air Staff at the Pentagon. He entered the U.S. Air Force in 2000 after graduating from the Air Force Academy. Major Leutner is an F-16 pilot and he has also served as an air liaison officer with the U.S. Army. He has air combat experience over Iraq and Libya and has worked in the U.S. Air Force's Central Combined Air and Space Operations Center. He is a 2013 graduate of the Marine Corps School of Advanced

Warfighting, and his professional interests include weapons of mass destruction studies, emerging airpower concepts/strategies, and deterrence theory.

Major August R. Immel graduated from the University of San Diego and was commissioned into the Marine Corps in May 1999. Major Immel is a combat engineer officer and holds additional military occupational specialties as a Latin American foreign area officer and MAGTF planner. He holds a bachelor's degree in history, an associate's degree in Spanish, and master's degrees in classical history, international studies, military studies, and operational studies.

Major Marcus J. Mainz is an infantry officer. He has commanded at the platoon and company level, including serving as a platoon commander for Company G, 2d Battalion, 7th Marines; combined antiarmor platoon commander for Weapons Company 2/7; and company commander for 3d Battalion, 7th Marines. At the Marine Corps Basic School in Quantico, Virginia, he served as a warfighting instructor, a staff platoon commander (Echo and India Companies), and an infantry officer course (IOC) instructor. His operational deployments include tours in ar-Ramadi, Iraq, for OIF 6-08 and AO West in support of OIF 8.2 under Regimental Combat Team 5 and 8. Currently Major Mainz is assigned as a planner for II MEF G-3 FOPS, Camp Lejeune, North Carolina. From July 2009 to July 2012, Mainz was an instructor at the Marine Corps Expeditionary Warfare School (EWS). He was responsible for revising and teaching the Command and Control Curriculum for the school, including the development of a new complex political, social, and military-focused exercise—New Dominion. He, Major Aaron Angell, and Lieutenant Colonel Brian H. Kane were the primary instructors for the Marine Corps Planning Process and Critical Thinking and they were instrumental in developing the concept of the Green Cell to account for cultural factors in planning. Mainz's contributions to the field of operational culture led to his role as coauthor of this edited volume.

Major Misty J. Posey is a Marine combat engineer officer with more than 14 years of service. She has commanded at the platoon and company level and has completed several deployments. She also served as the training officer for a Marine expeditionary unit and as the engineer officer with Tactical Training Exercise Control Group. She graduated from the University of San Diego in 1995 with a bachelor's degree in education. She is a recent graduate of the Marine Corps Command and Staff College, attaining a master's in military studies. Posey is also a recent graduate of the School of Advanced Warfighting, attaining a master's in advanced warfighting. Major Posey is currently assigned to Marine Corps Combat Development Center, Marine Corps Base, Quantico.

Major Nicholas Rose has served in Army and Joint Intelligence postings within the Australian Defence Force (ADF). He has deployed on a range of domestic Australian and overseas operations with the ADF, including deployments to Afghanistan and East Timor. He is a graduate of the Marine Corps Command and Staff College and the School of Advanced Warfighting. Rose is currently a plans officer within the Australian Defence Force Deployable Joint Force Headquarters.

Major Ryan D. Shea has served as an assistant supply officer for Headquarters Company, 1st Marine Regiment; supply officer for 2d Battalion, 1st Marines; operations officer and executive officer at Marine Corps Recruiting Station Fort Lauderdale, Florida; and supply officer and later support center director for 2d Marine Special Operations Battalion. Major Shea's deployments in support of combat operations include serving as the supply officer for the 15th Marine Expeditionary Unit, Battalion Landing Team 2/1, during OIF. Additionally, Shea supported OEF while serving as the support center director for Special Operations Task Force 82. He is currently deployed in support of OEF as the plans officer for Combat Logistics Regiment 2. He is a graduate of the Marine Corps Command and Staff College and the School of Advanced Warfighting. Major Shea's personal decorations include the Navy and Marine Corps Achievement Medal, gold star in lieu of second award; the Navy and a Marine Corps Commendation Medal with gold star in lieu of third award; and the Bronze Star. Shea is married to the former Janice Khreis and they have a daughter named Charlotte.

Major David Smith is a U.S. Army field artillery officer with combat tours in both Iraq and Afghanistan and two operational tours in South Korea. Major Smith commanded Alpha Battery, 2d Battalion, 17th Field Artillery, part of the 2d Infantry Brigade Combat Team, 2d Infantry Division, in Baghdad during OIF 06-08. Alpha Battery was re-tasked in a maneuver role during the 15-month deployment and was responsible for the al-Zafaraniyah District of southeast Baghdad. Major Smith is a 2012 graduate of the Air Force's Air Command and Staff College and a 2013 graduate of the Marine Corps School of Advanced Warfighting.

Major Jonathan R. Smith currently serves as the MAGTF planner for the MAGTF Staff Training Program. He is an infantry officer who has served as a weapons platoon commander; a platoon commander for 2d Reconnaissance Battalion; a commander for Fox Company, 2d Battalion, 4th Marines; and then as weapons company commander. During this time, he deployed twice to Iraq in support of OIF as well as to Liberia to conduct operations in support of Task Force Liberia. Following service as the officer in charge of the Basic Reconnaissance Course in Coronado, California, Major Smith took command of Marine Special Operations Company G, 2d Marine Special Operations Battalion. During his deployment to RC-West, Afghanistan, he was responsible for conducting village stability operations with six SOF teams in seven different village stability platforms. Major Smith is a graduate of the University of Maine and the Marine Corps School of Advanced Warfighting. His personal decorations include two Navy and Marine Corps Commendation Medals with Vs as well as two gold stars in lieu of fourth award; two Combat Action Ribbons; and the Lieutenant Colonel William G. Leftwich Jr. Award for outstanding leadership.

Lieutenant Commander Adam D. Wieder graduated from the U.S. Naval Academy in 1998 and commissioned into the surface warfare community. He served as the damage control assistant on the USS *Carney* (DDG 64) and as the ordnance officer on the USS *DeWert* (FFG 45), making a deployment on each ship to the Mediterranean. He returned to the Naval Academy and served in the Office of the Commandant of Midshipmen. Going back to sea, he served as the weapons officer and then as the combat systems officer aboard the USS *Shoup* (DDG 86), homeported in Everett, Washington State. While aboard the *Shoup*, Lieutenant Commander Wieder deployed to both the Western Pacific and the Central Command areas of responsibility. He selected into the missile defense specialty and subsequently served in the Forward Deployed Naval Forces on the U.S. 7th Fleet staff from 2009 to 2011 as the integrated air and missile defense plans officer. Lieutenant Commander Wieder's experiences during this tour, as well as the operational culture courses of instruction at the Marine Corps Command and Staff College (2011-12) and the School of Advanced Warfighting (2012-13), served as the foundation for his work. Wieder is currently assigned to the J3 at U.S. Central Command Headquarters.

Introduction

As the United States and its allies draw down from major combat operations in Iraq and Afghanistan, we have a unique opportunity to reflect upon the lessons we have learned in fighting wars that cannot be won through "conventional" means. In the past, U.S. political and military leaders have dismissed such conflicts as "irregular" and atypical, quickly returning to business as usual in their rush to forget wars that do not result in immediate and obvious success in the eyes of the public. Yet, unless we carefully record how our forces have adapted and learned from these conflicts, future generations will repeat the mistakes of their predecessors.

Perhaps one of the more controversial initiatives of the United States and its allies in response to the irregular warfare challenges in Afghanistan and Iraq has been the effort to incorporate cultural considerations into military planning and operations. Curiously, although "winning the hearts and minds" of the population has been a popular battle cry for the past decade, to date no research has actually documented or evaluated how and if military units actually adapted to cultural factors during operations. This volume of essays provides an important record of the cultural lessons learned during the past decade—not only in Afghanistan and Iraq but by military officers operating around the globe.

Case Studies in Operational Culture draws together the experiences of 22 field grade military officers from the U.S. Army, Navy, Air Force, and Marine Corps, as well as two of our military allies, Canada and Australia. Each of these officers has written a succinct summary of the cultural challenges that he or she faced in a previous operation, along with an explanation of the lessons learned as a result. Applying the cultural concepts described in two previous volumes in this series, *Operational Culture for the Warfighter* and *Applications in Operational Culture*, these essays provide detailed illustrations of how specific cultural factors had a direct impact on the success of military operations.

The cases that follow are grouped according to the cultural challenges faced by the authors and their units. Although the details of the specific challenges vary according to the country and region where the authors conducted their operations, these military officers all faced similar patterns of cultural challenges regardless of where they deployed. The cases illustrate an important point: the lessons learned can be applied to prepare for cultural challenges in future operations anywhere around the globe. Indeed, more than a quarter of the cases in this book focus on countries other than Iraq and Afghanistan—Ecuador, Thailand, Libya, Japan, and Australia—making a compelling argument that cultural understanding is not merely a skill required for the recent conflicts of OIF (Operation Iraqi Freedom) and OEF (Operation Enduring Freedom).

Illustrating this point, the first section focuses not on the cross-cultural challenges that military personnel faced interacting with foreign populations but on the cultural challenges the authors faced within their own military. As Major Nicholas Rose describes for the Australian military and Lieutenant Colonel David Aragon illustrates in his discussion of the cross-cultural differences between Air Force and SOF (Special Operations Forces), there are cross-cultural differences within one's own military that can influence unit cohesion and effectiveness.

Part two explores the many facets of working with local civilian populations. Major Clark Mitchell, Commander A. J. Kruppa, Major Bradley Bean, and Major Brandon Gordon each discuss the challenges of understanding how their military operations interrupted local economic activities. By restricting access to key aspects of the environment—such as water (Mitchell), food (Kruppa), transportation of goods (Bean), and movement within the area (Graham)—military operations may have potentially damaged relationships with the local population. The authors' explanations of how these problems were or were not resolved by their units provide important considerations for military members whose operations are likely to interrupt civilian activities in deployments around the world.

A second issue discussed by several of the authors is the challenge of working with key leaders in a foreign area of operation (AO). Lieutenant Colonel Justin Ansel and Majors David Smith, Llonie Cobb, and Jonathan Smith each explore the problems they faced when determining which individuals or groups were considered legitimate leaders in their AO. In all of the cases, the officers stressed the importance of understanding local political and social power structures. When resolving the cultural challenges in their AO, many of these authors emphasized stepping back to let the local population develop and apply their own solutions to the problems rather than enforcing Western methods and approaches.

For example, Major Carrie Batson describes how her unit was able to bring stability to the area and avoid religious tensions in the sacred city of an-Najaf, Iraq, by employing local Iraqis to defend the sacred Shi'ite Muslim shrine of Ali. Lieutenant Colonel Eric Dill explains how his team was able to resolve the problem presented by female detainees by working with local leaders and marrying the women into local families according to Iraqi Muslim custom: a solution that certainly runs contrary to American ideas of gender and marriage. Majors Misty Posey and Jason Borovies describe how their units adapted their operations to the gender ideals of the Muslim communities where they were operating, adjusting checkpoint procedures (Borovies) and the dress and movements of a female Marine (Posey). Finally, Major Corey Frederickson explains how efforts to obtain measures of assessment in Kandahar, Afghanistan, had to be revised to account for Afghan norms before the unit could obtain realistic data.

Part three examines a fascinating range of cross-cultural challenges in the joint operating environment. Paradoxically, while much of the cross-cultural training for the U.S. military has focused on success working with civilians on the ground, the reality is that many military leaders find working with their allies and military counterparts to be equally, if not more challenging. Majors Ryan Shea, Marcus Mainz, and John Gianopoulos provide detailed examples of the cultural challenges they each faced training and coordinating with local police and military forces in Iraq and Afghanistan. Illustrating the fact that challenges working with military partners were not limited to OEF and OIF, Major August Immel discusses his attempts to coordinate training and advising with the Ecuadorian military. Lieutenant Colonel Derek Brannon describes how cross-cultural misunderstandings severely hampered a multinational PACOM (Pacific Command) flight training exercise.

Major Steven Leutner provides a positive example of using cultural understanding to effectively include the Jordanian Air Force in Coalition operations against Libya.

Providing a fitting conclusion to the book, Lieutenant Commander Adam Wieder examines the strategic challenges of coordinating air and missile defense plans in the Pacific with the Japanese. Wieder's essay clearly illustrates the importance of understanding the historical and cultural perspectives of regional partners. He argues that cultural considerations are not merely a tactical concern focused on building good relations with local communities; indeed, they are critical if the United States and its allies hope to create effective plans and strategic solutions that depend upon the cooperation of culturally diverse partners in a region.

Part I:

Challenges Across
Service Cultures

Understanding the Environment and Social Structures: Keys to Accessing Indigenous Australian Communities for the Army

Major Nicholas Rose,
Australian Army

Aboriginal communities in northern Australia have conducted surveillance operations with the Australian Defence Force (ADF) since World War II.[1] Border protection operations[2] in the remote and sparsely populated areas of northern Australia are conducted routinely by Australian Army Regional Force Surveillance Units (RFSU)[3] with the assistance of indigenous Australians. Since the majority of the lands encompassed by these operations are traditional Aborigines and Torres Strait Islanders, each of the RFSU recruits trains and employs indigenous Australians, chiefly for their excellent local knowledge and bush skills.[4]

Cross-cultural challenges when conducting these operations have forced the ADF to acknowledge the importance of cultural knowledge when dealing with its own population. As the following case illustrates, understanding the cultural dimensions of social structure and the environment can be critical to resolving

---

[1] Amoury Vane, *North Australia Observer Unit–Unit History of an Army Surveillance Regiment* (Riverwood, NSW: Australian Military History Publications, 2000), 127-134.

[2] Australian Defence Force Border Protection operations are conducted as Operation Resolute and cover the entire economic exclusion zone (EEZ) on the continent of Australia. For more information, see Australian Defence Force, "Border Protection," http://www.defence.gov.au/op/borderprotection/general.htm.

[3] Regional Force Surveillance Units (RFSU) are Australian Army units dedicated to land-based regional surveillance operations in the north of Australia and include the North-West Mobile Force (NORFORCE); the 51st Battalion, Far North Queensland Regiment; and the Pilbara Regiment. Each unit recruits, trains, and employs local indigenous Australians as surveillance patrolmen to conduct their operations. For more information, see Australian Army, "Australian Army 6th Brigade," http://www.army.gov.au/Who-we-are/Divisions-and-Brigades/Forces-Command/6th-Brigade/North-West-Mobile-Force.

[4] Fraser and Rose, "A Short Guide to Training Indigenous Soldiers in the North-West Mobile Force (NORFORCE)," (Darwin, NT: Unofficial Australian Army Unit Publication, November 2000), 7.

seemingly intractable conflicts, even within one's own national borders.

During border protection actions in northern Australia in 1999, the Aboriginal community of Kalumburu[5] refused access to remote coastal lands and communities for the recruitment of local young men necessary for surveillance operations of illegal activities. As part of the operational plan, a dedicated local patrol was required for surveillance on the land surrounding Kalumburu, suspected of being a key location for these illegal activities. This land, however, was traditional Aboriginal land and contained a number of sacred sites, many of which were off-limits to outsiders of the local Gamberre tribal group.[6] Tribal elders had been angered by the lack of respect by the RFSU concerning access protocols to the community, which required face-to-face contact with elders rather than a phone call to the government-appointed community leader. As a result, an RFSU patrol had not been conducted in the area for more than eight years.

Access to traditional tribal land and communities by outsiders is a sensitive issue for Aboriginal people. The linkage of groups to their land is an essential component of their tribal identity and connection to the spiritual concept of "dreaming."[7] Sacred sites are also extremely sensitive areas relating to religious practices, such as coming of age ceremonies. Outsider access—from the elders' perspective—could have a serious impact on the sacredness of religious sites, contrary to the explicit law of the tribe. Restricted access to the land by local elders is an example of the

---

[5] Kalumburu is a small Aboriginal community located approximately 650 km west of Darwin and approximately 2,500 km northeast of Perth. It is the closest mainland settlement in Australia to Timor (including East Timor), Sumba (Indonesia), and the strategic Timor Sea Gas Field. Keith Lye, *Philip's Encyclopedic World Atlas* (London, UK: Octopus Publishing, 2002), 46-47.

[6] Gamberre is a northern Australian Aboriginal language group that includes the Cape Bougainville and Kalumburu areas. D. Horton, (ed.), *The Encyclopedia of Aboriginal Australia: Aboriginal and Torres Strait Islander History, Society and Culture*, (Darwin, NT: Australian Institute of Aboriginal and Torres Strait Islander Studies, Aboriginal Studies Press, 1994).

[7] Dreaming is ". . . an Aboriginal concept that can be seen as the embodiment of Aboriginal creation that gives meaning to everything; the essence of Aboriginal belief about creation, spiritual, and physical existence. It establishes the rules governing relationships between people, the land, and all things for Aboriginal people." Fraser, 5.

operational cultural dimension of the physical environment, specifically that of land ownership and religious symbolism associated to that land. The cultural taboos regarding the land are also an example of social mores (cultural rules or laws) within the dimension of belief systems, illustrating the fluid nature of operational culture themes. Additionally, the problem highlights the cultural dimension of social structures, namely deference to elders. Rather than going to "official" leaders within the community, community elders are often relied upon for key decisions, such as land access and the recruitment of young men for army service.

To resolve the problem, leaders of the RFSU approached community elders in person to first discuss past practices of the unit without raising land access issues. While the current RFSU leaders were not responsible for past actions, they apologized for those of their predecessors. The humble approach found favor with the elders, who then explained the importance of their land with respect to detecting illegal activities. RFSU fostered this relationship in dealings over a period of four weeks, which included many more meetings to discuss the benefits of army service and RFSU plans, highlighting the critical role the elders had to play— selecting suitable young men for the patrol.

Finally, the RFSU proposed a solution: they would work with the elders to raise a local patrol consisting of Aboriginal men and led by an Aboriginal officer. This plan would allow access to the area for surveillance by a lawful tribal member and aid the patrol in avoiding specific sacred sites or denigrating local customs. The community elders approved this plan, and a successful patrol was raised. The positive benefits of army service for the local indigenous communities also generated additional recruits for the unit, allowing the RFSU to support wider operations and highlighting a second-order effect of the applications of cultural understanding.

The process of building relationships between RFSU leaders and tribal elders in Kalumburu demonstrates how military personnel must consider the dimensions of operational culture as a whole so as to not miss linked themes with operational implications. Effective leadership, detailed knowledge of local cultural issues, the ability to learn and adapt, and an understanding of who can deal humbly and patiently with local indigenous elders are all vital for successful operations. Through such personal interactions, many instances of cross-cultural miscommunication can be avoided.

The Challenge of Surviving
within the Special Operations Culture

Lieutenant Colonel David K. Aragon,
U.S. Air Force

The culture of Special Operations Forces (SOF) consists of behavior and characteristics that would make any conventionally trained airman fearful of a court-martial. These were my thoughts during the summer of 2008 when I departed U-28A qualification at Hurlburt Field, Florida, and began my journey to Afghanistan as a member of a SOF team. The next several months were filled with individual and group actions that I, as a seasoned B-52 WSO (weapons systems officer), would reject outright at any other point in my career. As I discovered, integration into the SOF community was a cross-cultural operational challenge located *within* my own service. The following outlines my experience, analyzing the challenges through three lenses: the SOF social structure, political structure, and belief system.

Most aviators within the U.S. Air Force social structure share the belief that rank conveys specific customs and courtesies to be exercised while in the office. However, once inside the cockpit, rank is dismissed and the relationship hierarchy is based on who is the aircraft commander or mission commander. In the SOF community, rank is loosely coupled with authority, while experience within the unit often defined who is in charge, at least informally. Additional SOF characteristics such as their dismissal of standardized uniform wear and unit patches, while typical for my joint task force (JTF), were nevertheless a shock to my sense of normality. Furthermore, my previous experience in the B-52 community instilled in me an appreciation for operating within a fiscally constrained environment, whereas SOF appeared to be immersed in unlimited financial resources. This perception was reinforced by the $6,000 worth of gear issued to me while within the JTF—much of which went unused.

The SOF political structure also contrasted starkly with my previous experiences in the Air Force. Our JTF chain of command did not follow a rigid organizational chart template that I had accepted as standard throughout my career. Our relationships with various organizations fell along blurred and sometimes nonexistent lines that could not be readily defined as TACON (tactical control), OPCON (operational control), or COCOM (combatant command). Our chain of command and approval authorities often resided with whoever our "customer" was on a particular day. Sometimes it was another U.S. military unit or often an ally or other governmental agency. Up to this point, my experience had always involved answering to the Combined Forces Air Component Commander (CFACC), who in turn worked for the Joint Force Commander. In contrast, our JTF organization never conferred with the Combined Air Operations Center, a mainstay in the conventional Air Force world.

Finally, the SOF belief system was founded on a history of innovators and mavericks who challenged the established order of their own Services and broke with their paradigms to develop solutions to wicked problems. The B-52 community from which I came proudly traced its roots to Strategic Air Command and General Curtis E. LeMay. In short, I was categorized as a product of "Big Blue," the conventional or traditional arm of the Air Force. The SOF aviators I worked with seemingly thumbed their noses at the institutions I had proudly risen through over the years.

On more than one occasion, this behavior led to friction with my new peer group. For example, my adherence to strict rules of engagement (ROE) coupled with various instructions and directives dictating how to employ my aircraft. The SOF U-28A community at that time was not bound by such stringent rules, causing a great deal of anxiety almost every time I flew during the first few weeks. It was not until the end of my tour that our unit received its first formalized Air Force Instruction (AFI). Even then, despite my familiarity with the document, it was viewed by SOF aviators with a suspicious eye.

In the end, I was able to draw on my B-52 experience and apply several techniques to how I operated within the U-28A, leading to numerous tactical and operational successes on the battlefield. In turn, when I resumed my duties in "Big Blue," I reflected on my SOF experience and applied several lessons learned to enlighten my own tribe. I am now able to synthesize experiences from vastly different organizations into solutions for future air operations.

Part II

**Cross-Cultural Challenges
when Working with the
Local Civilian Population**

Operational Culture Challenge: Fallujah Peninsula, Iraq

Major Clark Mitchell,
U.S. Marine Corps

The Fallujah Peninsula lies directly east of the Euphrates River and due west of the city of Fallujah in Iraq. In 2007, I was the commander for Company A, 1st Battalion, 1st Marines, where we were given battle space that covered the Fallujah Peninsula area of operations (AO). This battle space had previously been in a region where the Iraq insurgency was prevalent. The unit had just completed a strong predeployment training cycle to prepare for a seven-month deployment, and I believed that Company A was ready for a successful tour of duty.

As we settled into our new battle space, however, there was an issue that required our immediate attention before the situation worsened. During counterinsurgency operations, the company was at risk of detonating improvised explosive devices (IEDs) placed by the local population. The root cause of this insurgent activity can be linked directly to two operational culture dimensions described in *Operational Culture for the Warfighter*: the physical environment and the economy of a culture.

On the peninsula, agriculture dominated the economy. In addition, the community's social structure was based on a tribal system. The local Abu Risha tribe was Sunni in origin and egalitarian by nature as reflected in its practice of communal distribution of goods and services, including water. Farming in the river valley has been a way of life for many of the Iraqi people whose families have lived on the peninsula for generations. Farmers who lived on the peninsula were dependent upon the water that the Euphrates River contributed to their crops. These crops provided bartering items and food for the farmer's extended family, which included many other members of the local Sunni tribe.

Because the Euphrates River was not regulated, the farmers could not reliably deliver enough water to their crops. To irrigate their fields, the farmers used pumping stations. These pumping stations would work so well that they would flood fields adjacent to the Euphrates River, which made it difficult for U.S. Marines to patrol the area. To deal with this problem, Marines on patrol from combat outposts nearby the river had persuaded the farmers to stop running their pumping stations. However, farmers in the tribe relied heavily on water to better their standards of life and to breathe life into their local economy through the sale of their produce. We did not understand the intimate relationship between this community and its environment, leading to unintended consequences.

During a two week relief-in-place with the former company, I was fortunate to meet and begin building relationships with the local tribal leaders in the community. Sheikh Khamis al-Hasnawi, who was the lead sheikh for the Abu Risha tribe on the peninsula, explained the local economy and the social structure of his tribe to me during our second meeting. This information was presented to me by Sheikh Khamis through an interpreter that the sheikh trusted, so I took it as important environmental information.

As Marines in Company A started uncovering improvised explosive devices (IEDs) on a main supply route in our battle space, this conversation with Sheikh Khamis proved integral in solving the IED threat problem. Knowing that Sheikh Khamis was a local leader and held an important symbolic place in the social structure, I visited with the sheikh to explain the company's situation concerning the recently emplaced IEDs.

The next morning, Sheikh Khamis held a *shura* (council meeting) with community leaders to conduct business and listen to complaints from the locals. Through this tribal *shura*, we discovered the connection between the IEDs placed in our battle space and the fact that peninsula crops were not receiving enough water. Farmers on the peninsula were starting to lose their crops since they could no longer use their pumping stations to flood their land. In retaliation for the Marines regulating the farmers' pumping stations, the local people had returned to insurgent ways, setting IEDs on road networks to gain our attention. Later that day, Sheikh Khamis and I formally apologized to each farmer and assisted the community in restarting the water pumping stations to flood their fields.

During overseas deployments, recognizing the importance of relevant factors within the physical environment and the economy of a foreign culture can resolve future conflicts with local populations. It is equally important to establish partnerships with local recognized leaders early in the deployment that will result in achieving campaign goals and prove beneficial to our operational success.

Operational Culture Onboard the al-Basrah Oil Terminal

Lieutenant Commander A. J. Kruppa
U.S. Navy

For six months in 2010, I joined a Coalition maritime task force on-board the Iraqi al-Basrah Oil Terminal (ABOT) to continue maritime security interoperability and execute a phased transition of responsibility to the Iraqi Navy. The Coalition's efforts during my time focused on point defense and maritime security, while developing robust training in maritime interdiction and vessel inspection procedures for the Iraqi Marines. These efforts were repeatedly delayed or disrupted due to a cultural misunderstanding by Coalition members regarding the local fishing economy and the physical environment surrounding ABOT.

ABOT is one of two Iraqi waterborne oil terminals in the northern Arabian Sea. On any given day, it had up to four supertankers berthed, onloading Iraqi crude oil and providing approximately 85 percent of Iraq's gross domestic product (GDP). In addition to Coalition civil-military partners and 20 Pakistani food-service contractors, every three weeks more than 100 Iraqi civilian workers and 30 Iraqi Marines were rotated into the terminal.

The terminal is located in the marshy al-Faw Peninsula along the Shatt al-Arab waterway—the entrance to Iraq's main port in al-Basrah. Due to this position, ABOT's surrounding waters are busy with hundreds of local fishermen and waterborne commerce (via *dhows*, or traditional sailing vessels) traveling in and around the vicinity of Iraqi and Iranian coasts. These vessels posed obvious security concerns. However, by regulating the vessels' activities around ABOT, most Coalition members did not realize that they were also damaging the fishing economy of the area.

Given the currents, depth, and seabed composition, the immediate ABOT area was known by locals as a hotbed for Iraq's fishing staple—the *hammour* (or grouper). Hammour is regionally valued and an important part of trade for fisherman in the al-Faw

Peninsula. These fish are considered groupers (bottom feeders) and, in the eyes of many Western military members, a substandard food. As a result, security operations required to defend the terminal and conduct vessel interdiction tended to ignore the importance of local fishing spots. Instead, military efforts focused on maintaining a security barrier around the terminal.

As Coalition members conducted oversight on vessel boarding procedures demonstrated by Iraqi Marines, they would provide negative grades when the marines did not communicate to fisherman that they must leave the area. Although Coalition members stressed the importance of keeping locals far from the terminal, Iraqi Marines were routinely observed to be "complacent" or glib in their vessel visits. In reality, when the marines were observed to be "dragging on in meaningless fishing discussion" (instead of focusing on security information gathering), they were actually gathering valuable information. Their discussions revealed that the locals felt that security forces were disrespectful of their fishing livelihood and did not understand the maritime commerce value of the hammour.

Iraqi Marines did not agree with Coalition notions that the local fishermen were conducting maritime commerce as an informal (and therefore unimportant) economy. Instead, the Iraqi Marines accepted both unidentified and unregistered fishermen as important elements in the Iraqi maritime domain and economy. Yet the frame of Coalition success centered on restricting access to fishing grounds and stressed thorough documentation, inspection, and further punitive measures.

Attempts by Iraqi Marines to meet Coalition standards were not received well by locals, as they displayed an unwillingness to share information about important security issues or to build further relationships with the security forces. Furthermore, Coalition training rubrics resulted in a negative narrative to locals that Iraqi Marines were working with the Coalition military to control and limit access to food and degrade the fishing economy.

This situation had a gradual resolution during my time onboard, as more outspoken, newly reported (locally raised) Iraqi Marine officers were willing to share their values with Coalition members.

16

These new Iraqis stressed the importance of respecting local fishing practices. They made continued suggestions both to training supervisors and, eventually, the Coalition task force commander to allow Iraqi Marines leniency on their methods as a means to improve results.

This dialogue was starting to occur as I departed. In fact, prior to Iraq's transfer of full control of ABOT, Coalition members concluded that an Iraqi maritime cultural-acceptance model was valuable and critical to maritime security cooperation. These experiences illustrate the importance of understanding the differing values of food around the world and the varying methods used in their collection and distribution. Future maritime forces can benefit from these lessons through classroom and predeployment discussions on the food (fish) economies in varying littoral regions.

Operational Culture Impacts in Rutbah, Iraq

Major Bradley P. Bean,
U.S. Marine Corps

From 2006 to 2007, a Marine expeditionary unit (MEU) took part in the "surge" of U.S. Forces in Iraq. A significant portion of the unit was assigned to clear Rutbah and reestablish security in the city and the surrounding area. After success in the initial clearing operations, a necessary follow-up operation was to isolate Rutbah from the insurgents. To accomplish this, Coalition forces isolated the city by constructing a large earthen berm around Rutbah and creating vehicle checkpoints on all roads entering the city, preventing insurgents from transiting to and from the city freely. Isolating the city had direct second- and third-order effects, both economically and on how the population interacted with the environment.

Unbeknownst to the MEU at the time, these effects could have been prevented if the MEU staff had obtained a better understanding of the uniqueness of Rutbah and its population. Isolating the city had a significant economic impact on both the insurgents and on the entire population. It was not until an extensive census was conducted and civil-military operations began that the unit fully realized the hardships it had inadvertently created on the populace.

Rutbah was a unique area with its own formal and informal economy that differed from other areas the Marines had dealt with in western al-Anbar Province. This difference was not apparent early on during the operations. Rutbah sits on a major road near the Syrian border in southwest Iraq. This main road and the economy were directly linked to each other. Many businesses and both the formal and an informal economy relied on transporting goods across the border from Syria into Iraq and vice versa. Due to the location of Rutbah, most traffic in and out of Syria would come through the city, providing a key source of goods and income for the citizens of Rutbah. The informal economy mainly consisted of goods smuggled across the Iraq/Syria border. The Marine units assigned to the area did not immediately understand the extent to which most of the population of Rutbah relied on external sources and imports from other areas, to include items from the informal economy. This would have been important knowledge for commanders to consider when initially making decisions.

The problems caused by the vehicle checkpoints and the berm were most apparent in their effects on the economy and population. These measures prevented essential items, such as kerosene and gas, from getting in and out of the city. Even though the fuel situation had always been unpredictable, the vehicle checkpoints and berm exacerbated the situation. During the cold winter season, the shortage of fuels to heat homes and to cook food caused some undue suffering that quickly needed to be rectified. The fuel shortage caused the Marines to lose credibility and legitimacy with some citizens. As a result, kerosene and gas were allowed to enter the city again. It then had to be more closely regulated to prevent severe price inflation because of the shortage.

Essential services in the city, such as trash collection, also ceased because of a shortage of the trucks, equipment, and trained personnel who were prevented from entering and leaving the city on a regular schedule. Trash piled up in random areas of the town, creating an unhealthy environment and an unbearable smell in many neighborhoods. In retrospect, if an established plan would have been put in place for these inevitable occurrences, the Marines might have gained more credibility initially among the population they were trying to secure and influence.

Overall, however, the Marines did things right and had a highly successful tour. Although the steps taken to counter the insurgency were essential at the time, a better understanding of the nuances of the Rutbah culture, specifically the economy and the physical environment, could have prevented some unnecessary problems. This understanding cannot be just a rudimentary understanding for a few in a unit. Everyone interacting with the population needs to understand the various nuances.

Just like each country is unique in its cultures and beliefs, each city is also unique. Realizing that the citizens of Rutbah were reliant on both the formal and the informal economy for their livelihood would have been the first step. By better understanding the cultural environment, specifically the importance and significance of the road that Rutbah was located on, decisions could have been made earlier to prevent such a severe impact on the population. The decisions made after the clearing of Rutbah had direct impacts for months, and may have prevented some of the likely "fence sitters" in the population from siding with the Coalition earlier than they eventually did.

Solving the Terrain Denial Dilemma in al-Anbar Province

Major Brandon W. Graham
U.S. Marine Corps

In an eastern sector of al-Anbar Province, Iraq, in early 2006, 1st Battalion, 1st Marines, was clearing enemy forces while simultaneously building relations with the local population. The battalion's area of operations (AO) was significant in size; its enormity prevented friendly forces from patrolling the AO's entirety on a continuous basis. The resulting gap between the assigned area and forces available allowed for enemy forces to launch indirect fire attacks with relative impunity. The enemy effectively targeted combat outposts and semi-permanent patrol bases throughout the AO on a regular basis. The situation presented a dilemma for 1st Battalion, 1st Marines: the battalion had to stop these indirect attacks, but it had to do so in a manner that would not impair relations with the population.

To examine the dilemma through an operational culture perspective, one can look through two lenses of cultural dimension as identified in *Operational Culture for the Warfighter*. The first dimension is the physical environment. In considering response options, the battalion studied the specifics of the attacks and successfully determined multiple geographic points-of-origin (POO) for the enemy missions. The battalion's local units explored the land surrounding these POO sites through aerial imagery and ground reconnaissance and determined the proximity of culturally sensitive sites as well as civilian infrastructure. Additionally, the on-scene units also noted the locals' use of the land, which leads to the second lens of examination: the economy of a culture.

In defining the economy of a culture, *Operational Culture for the Warfighter* states that "All cultural groups have a specific system [an economy of culture] for obtaining, producing, and distributing items (food, clothing, cars, houses, etc.) and services (medical care, education, etc.) that people need or want to survive in their society."[8] This system also factored into the response options considered by the battalion. After significant information gathering, 1st Battalion, 1st Marines' units found that the local population used much of the land encompassing the POO sites for agrarian purposes. The battalion subsequently determined that if it was to avoid damaging relations with the locals, it had to address the threat in a way that would have minimal impact on the local economy and people's livelihood.

The battalion chose to employ terrain denial fires—systematic use of observed indirect fires against the POO sites—to address the threat. To ensure that the battalion did not damage relations with the local population, it implemented stringent collateral damage estimates (i.e., the battalion extended the minimum safe distances between impacts and infrastructure/livestock beyond theater requirements, and the observer canceled the mission if any civilians were near the site). Additionally, the battalion requested settings on munitions that would minimize damage to the land (e.g., variable time fuses). Furthermore, to promote relations with the populace, terrain denial missions were coordinated with transparent messaging operations directed at the locals. Ultimately, the terrain denial missions proved effective. The number of indirect fire attacks declined significantly in the AO and, possibly most promising, the population noted that the enemy presence in the area had declined as a result.

This vignette demonstrates the value of considering operational culture while developing military courses of action. The 1st Battalion, 1st Marines, did not necessarily use the terminology outlined in this case, but the battalion understood the importance and potential impacts of its actions on the broader mission. As such, the battalion developed an effective program to solve its terrain denial dilemma while maintaining its long-term objectives.

---

[8] Barak A. Salmoni and Paula Holmes-Eber, *Operational Culture for the Warfighter: Principles and Application* (Quantico, VA: Marine Corps University Press, 2011), 79.

The Successful Application
of Operational Culture Dimensions
in an-Najaf, Iraq

Major Carrie C. Batson,
U.S. Marine Corps

In August 2004, my unit—the 11th Marine Expeditionary Unit (11th MEU)—became engaged in major combat operations in the holy Shia city of an-Najaf, Iraq. After three weeks of fighting against radical cleric Muqtada al-Sadr and his *Mahdi Militia*, a cease-fire agreement was reached. While the 11th MEU celebrated the conclusion of fighting, it now faced an even tougher challenge: how to return long-term stability to the populous city. The MEU took numerous steps to resolve this problem. Three actions addressed the operational culture dimensions of: 1) physical environment, 2) belief systems, and 3) economy.

The physical environment dimension includes the symbolic significance of land. Like many cities considered holy by the world's religions, an-Najaf is a holy place for Shia Muslims for several reasons. First among these is the presence of the Imam Ali Shrine, where Prophet Muhammad's son-in-law and the first Shi'a imam, Ali, is buried. The shrine is located in the *medina*, the city's historic center, where al-Sadr's political office is also located. Although the MEU kept a permanent presence in the medina during the fighting against the insurgents, the MEU commander decided to limit the Marines' post-hostilities presence to prevent further animosity by the local population. Instead, the MEU decided to train Iraqi soldiers and police to patrol the area and ensure al-Sadr's compliance with the cease-fire agreement. While this decision was not without some risk, since the nascent Iraqi troops would be ill prepared to handle a confrontation with the *Mahdi Militia* if al-Sadr chose to order it, the MEU commander understood that such a risk was necessary to gain and maintain the population's support.

The operational culture dimension of belief systems involves honor codes that often "provide a basis for assumptions" about how someone will interpret and respond to events. In Iraq, this behavior code involves the need to avenge an injustice if a person is to restore his or her honor. During the three weeks of combat in an-Najaf, some of the local population suffered property damage, personal injury, or death of a loved one due to U.S. and *Mahdi Militia* actions. Understanding that an-Najafis would feel compelled to avenge what they believed to be injustices, the MEU implemented the first use of solatia, or condolence payments, in Iraq. One day a week at the an-Najaf governor's compound, aggrieved members of the local population were encouraged to bring a file documenting their case. Marine "judges" then would adjudicate these cases to determine if compensation would be given, and if so, how much. Not only did solatia end the need for revenge, but it also built lasting trust with the local populace.

Economy, another operational culture dimension, involves both formal and informal economic systems. After combat operations ceased in an-Najaf, the MEU initiated several projects to strengthen the city's formal economic system and its ability to secure revenue. One project involved hiring local an-Najafi contractors to rebuild outdoor markets that had been destroyed in the fighting and to build new markets in areas of need. While these markets were built with MEU funds, the local government "owned" and rented them at reasonable prices to local merchants. This revenue stream increased the government's ability to provide its citizens with essential services and welfare assistance, which in turn increased the government's legitimacy in the people's eyes and reduced al-Sadr's influence in the city.

These examples provide a glimpse of a much larger and comprehensive MEU plan to bring lasting security and prosperity to an-Najaf. In hindsight, it is remarkable that the MEU, working alongside the nascent local Iraqi government, was able to conceive of and implement such a plan before "counterinsurgency" or "operational culture" concepts had regained popularity in the U.S. military. This feat is even more remarkable considering that less than a year after fighting had ceased, the MEU transferred control of an-Najaf back to the Iraqis. An-Najaf was a success story then and remains a stable and prosperous city to this day.

Key Leader Engagement

By, With, and Through:
Working with a Neighborhood Council

Major David Smith
U.S. Army

In 2007, the 2d Infantry Brigade Combat Team assumed responsibility for security in southeast Baghdad. As part of this effort, Alpha Battery 2-17th Field Artillery was assigned the al-Zafaraniyah neighborhood along the Tigris River. The area of operation consisted of 13 *mulhallas* represented by an elected Neighborhood Advisory Council or NAC. The local NAC were part of a political stratification that had been imposed by Coalition forces in 2003.[9] As the commander responsible for managing al-Zafaraniyah, I was required to work with the NACs to establish local governance despite suspicions of corruption.[10]

Over the 15 months that Alpha Battery operated in al-Zafaraniyah, battery leadership had to interact with the NAC on a wide range of issues from security to governance. In one particular case, which involved planning the distribution of humanitarian aid to an impoverished mulhalla, an initial misunderstanding of the NAC's social and political structure and roles within the community resulted in an event that came close to becoming a serious incident.

Political structure can be defined as, "The way that power and leadership are apportioned to people, and exercised, according to the social structure of the society."[11] As a political construct, the NAC was new to the people of al-Zafaraniyah. In place since late 2003, the NAC system had been imposed on the city of Baghdad by Coalition forces. The common perception upon my arrival was that the NAC was an artificial construct that was not embraced by the local population. In addition, the al-Zafaraniyah area was pre-

---

[9] Salmoni and Holmes-Eber, 154.
[10] The al-Zafaraniyah NAC consisted of 13 members, all elected, which represented each of the neighborhoods. Most members had been in the job since late 2003, although some had been killed by insurgents and were replaced. The head of each NAC in Baghdad represented their district in the district advisory council or DAC.
[11] Salmoni and Holmes-Eber, 153.

dominantly Shi'a Muslim and was thoroughly linked to the *Jaysh al-Mahdi* (JAM) militia, the major insurgent group in east Baghdad.[12] My initial view of the NAC, therefore, was that they were ineffectual, corrupt, and potentially supporting the enemy.[13]

Of all the neighborhoods in al-Zafaraniyah, Mulhalla 979 was a major concern because it was the most poverty stricken. Patrols had spoken with the locals and many claimed they had received no help from the local government. I was determined to help these people and felt that I could not trust the NAC to ensure aid reached Mulhalla 979 since the NAC had diverted aid to family and friends in the past.[14] The small combined force of Alpha Battery and Iraqi Army soldiers moved into 979 and established a perimeter while an interpreter broadcast our intent to provide aid to the community. Within minutes, the area was surrounded by several hundred locals and all semblance of order was lost.[15] The supplies were distributed in a haphazard manner and many people had to leave empty handed. My Iraqi Army counterparts commented afterward that even in Iraq "this was not how you do this."

After the event, I struggled with what had gone so wrong. I realized that I did not understand the social/political structure, how the NAC really functioned in al-Zafaraniyah, or how they could enable my mission.[16] The NAC were the only formal leaders in al-Zafaraniyah and, as a result, understood the mulhallas in ways I never

---

[12] The JAM militia used al-Zafaraniyah as a staging area to launch attacks into contested areas of Baghdad. Most of the Sunni population had been driven out by terror tactics in 2005. All of the NAC members were Shia and intelligence pointed to the fact that they had contact with JAM. JAM represented a "shadow" government that all local leaders had to acknowledge if they were to survive.

[13] Many of my opinions regarding the NAC were formed during the relief in place–transition of authority (RIP TOA) with the outgoing unit from the 101st Airborne. They had not worked much with the NAC and had little good to say other than that they were all on the "target list" as potential enemies to detain. After I had matured in the AO, it became evident that the previous unit had not had much engagement with the NAC and therefore did not know who they were dealing with.

[14] On previous occasions, the NAC members had tried to divert contracts or aid to their relatives or to the neighborhoods they represented.

[15] With only a single strand of wire in place, the small perimeter containing the trucks with the aid and the security force was quickly surrounded by a large crowd that began pressing up against the wire.

[16] Salmoni and Holmes-Eber, 110.

could.[17] Two months after that chaotic aid distribution, I was able to obtain another truckload of blankets, heating oil, and food. This time, I chose to work with and through the NAC, allowing them to plan and supervise the aid drop. I put myself in an enabling role for manpower and security. The results could not have been more different. The NAC advertised the drop weeks in advance and all of the mulhallas were notified of the place and time of the event. The NAC used the council hall government center as the distribution point.[18] This allowed for greatly increased organization and security. The Iraqi Army was able to use ID card checks to ensure everyone went through the line only once.[19]

In the end, the second drop was a compromise. I was not able to achieve my original intent of targeting just 979 and had to accept the fact that some NAC favoritism was going to play into the drop. I realized, however, that as the political leaders, the NAC had to live with their actions and had to answer to the people if corruption and favoritism was apparent. I also learned that a NAC solution to an Iraqi problem would almost always be better than anything I could manage on my own in al-Zafaraniyah. It was their country and their government system.

---

[17] Patrols brought back mixed reporting throughout the year from people on the street regarding the NACs. We would ask if people know who they were and if they had seen them in the neighborhood lately. The overall trend was in favorable reporting, but it was obvious that the NACs were not known by all and had a tendency to keep to the council hall.
[18] Salmoni and Holmes-Eber, 114. The use of the government building served to reinforce the idea that the NAC were the political leaders and that their workplace was the center of power in al-Zafaraniyah.
[19] Several tons of supplies were distributed and the operation was not only a social and political success but an information operations opportunity to highlight NACs in action for the media.

The Cultural Grounds
of the Delaram Gravel Conflict

Major Llonie A. C. Cobb
U.S. Marine Corps

Early one morning in March 2010, the American owner of a trucking company, Mr. Smith (the gentleman's real name eludes me) came to the main entrance of Forward Operating Base (FOB) Delaram II, Afghanistan, requesting to see the camp commander. Mr. Smith was escorted to the Regimental Combat Team (RCT) 2 "Shura Dome" (conference room), where the RCT-2 executive officer (XO), operations officer, air officer, intelligence officer, and Afghan National Army liaison officer were waiting. During the subsequent hour, Mr. Smith detailed how the previous night, two "Taliban" members broke into his living quarters and threatened to kill him unless he fired his current employees, hired individuals they designated, and paid a "tax" to one of the local strongmen. While it is easy to categorize the aforementioned encounter as extortion based on avarice, closer inspection would reveal this encounter to be the result of inadvertent cultural transgressions in the economic and social structure dimensions of operational culture.[20]

Mr. Smith was contracted to provide gravel to FOB Delaram II, which was still under construction while occupied by RCT-2 and the 2/215th ANA Brigade. Lacking an understanding of the cultural dynamics of Delaram, Mr. Smith directly hired the required number of laborers and commenced dredging the Khash Rud River and delivering the gravel to FOB Delaram II. Almost immediately, Mr. Smith and his employees became the target of "harassment." One vehicle was stolen and, on several occasions, he received sporadic rifle fire on the jobsite. Other than randomly shifting the times and locations for his dredging operations, Mr. Smith made no effort to resolve this situation. After he was threatened, however, he solicited a military resolution from RCT-2, figuring the FOB's gravel requirement would nudge the regiment into swift military action on

---

[20] Salmoni and Holmes-Eber, 51.

his behalf. He was right, but the regiment's response was not what he expected.

Drawing on cultural training received prior to deployment and the relationship the regiment enjoyed with the Delaram district elders, the RCT's command immediately recognized that Mr. Smith's first transgression was in the economic dimension. Perhaps more than other Afghan districts, Delaram's economy, both formal and informal,[21] was well defined. Its location at the intersection of four major roads and its bustling bazaar had contributed to stratifying the citizenry economically, the top strata being occupied by the land and business owners through whom most economic exchanges (primarily reciprocal and symbolic)[22] occur. By directly hiring labor, Mr. Smith subverted the established system and, thereby, incurred the wrath of the district strongman.

Mr. Smith's actions also constituted a transgression in the social structure dimension. The strongman's position and status[23] within the district allowed him to distribute wealth and favors amongst his kin. By directly hiring labor, the American contractor denied the strongman a privilege accorded to someone of his position. Further, he effectively usurped the strongman's authority. Naturally, the strongman felt insulted and justified in his attacks against Mr. Smith and his employees.

In the end, the situation was resolved through diplomatic and military means. RCT-2 requested a shura (council meeting) with the district chief and elders during which Mr. Smith agreed to add some recommended employees to his roster. Militarily, the 2/215th ANA Brigade began to patrol in the vicinity of Mr. Smith's dredging operations to ensure that harassment had, in fact, ended. Ultimately, the lesson learned by Mr. Smith and reinforced for RCT-2 was the prudence of consulting the local elders prior to recruiting labor or introducing wealth into the local economy. Moving without the consent of the elders could upset the power balance and bring about undesired angst.

---

[21] Ibid., 74-75.
[22] Salmoni and Holmes-Eber, 89-93.
[23] Ibid., 103-104.

An Angry Crowd:
Operational Culture in Musa Qala, Afghanistan

Lieutenant Colonel Justin J. Ansel Jr.
U.S. Marine Corps

Shortly before 1st Battalion, 8th Marines, deployed to Afghanistan, a new district governor, Haji Namatula, took office in Musa Qala. Although Haji Namatula was now the formally designated head, in reality, numerous groups and individuals in the area still held and competed for informal power over the district. As this case illustrates, by understanding and working with both the formal and informal political structures in Musa Qala, 1st Battalion, 8th Marines, was able to diffuse a highly volatile situation and strengthen effective leadership in the community.

Upon its arrival, the battalion found a mostly hostile environment. Working in partnership with an Afghan National Army (ANA) battalion, 1st Battalion, 8th Marines, began offensive operations to clear the district center and surrounding areas of Taliban fighters. Both units worked hard to mitigate collateral damage, both human and materiel, which established credibility among the local population and pushed active Taliban membership outside Musa Qala's city limits.

Despite these efforts to reduce collateral damage, the Taliban began an information campaign to convince the locals of considerable causalities resulting from Marine and ANA actions. With rumors running rampant, the outlying villages sent representatives to the district center. Despite the ANA battalion commander's attempt to resolve the situation, the angry band, which was comprised mostly of Alizai tribesmen, demanded an audience with the Marine commander, with the impression that the Marines were the power brokers in Musa Qala.

The eldest tribesman, Haji Mazor Rackham (name changed), emerged as the representative for the group and adamantly demanded an audience with Marine leadership. The executive officer

(XO) noticed that Haji Rackham sat in a position of honor with the ANA personnel. Recognizing the important role of elders in Afghan social structure, the XO immediately began to form a relationship and listened as Haji Rackham expressed the concerns of the crowd.

The disgruntled group may have been acephalous (without a formal head), but Haji Rackham made a conscious decision to accept the responsibility for the crowd. He voluntarily took the grievance to Coalition forces, although he held no clear formal control or authority over the group. Using traditional means of conflict resolution, Haji Rackham attempted to adjudicate the complaints and concerns of the crowd by meeting with Coalition forces.

Once the XO and Haji Rackham reached an acceptable understanding, the next step was to address the angry crowd. Because a public display of authority and power was critical to men of Musa Qala, the XO escorted Haji Rackham to the crowd with a traditional Afghan handhold. As soon as they reached the crowd, Haji Rackham addressed the crowd before the XO could speak; in essence, Haji Rackham used his informal leadership within the Alizai tribe to advance the Coalition cause. Since Haji Rackham was of the same tribe as most of the people gathered, he shared a common ancestral bond that enabled effective communication with the angry crowd.

Next, relying upon an intuitive understanding of the social and political structure, the battalion XO effectively connected the informal leadership of the angry band of Alizais with the formal leadership of the new district governor, Haji Namatula. To do this, the XO referred Haji Rackham to the new district governor's office to resolve the grievance, reinforcing the formal political structure.

This case offers an important lesson in working with local leadership in an area of operations. Despite the XO's strong desire to be part of the solution, Afghans—both the formal and informal leadership—best handled this situation. Ultimately, it was not the battalion XO, but the Afghan leadership—namely Haji Namatula and Haji Rackham—that resolved the group's concerns. As the two leaders worked together to address the issues, the community began to meld the traditional complaint process with the contemporary formal complaint process.

Clearly, it is important for deploying Marines to understand the cultural dynamics of the operating environment. By intuitively working with existing social and political structures, the XO reduced the expectation to resolve issues via the Coalition force chain of command. However, in future operations, a comprehensive knowledge of existing social and political structures could replace this intuition.

Dynamic Dimensions of Dar-I-Bum

Major Jonathan R. Smith
U.S. Marine Corps

Dar-I-Bum (DIB) is a village situated within a fertile valley located in the center of Badghis Province, Afghanistan. During a recent deployment, the village was transformed from an insurgent safe-haven into an example of stability. Although that stability remains fragile, it offers a good case study highlighting the relevance of "cultural dimensions" as explained in *Operational Culture for the Warfighter*. This essay will focus on the political dimensions of culture, explaining how they were relevant in DIB and what lessons could be learned from the operation.

In 2011, DIB was selected as the site for village stability operations (VSO). U.S. troops were assigned to the area with the goal of implementing a multidimensional approach to stability. Dar-I-Bum was considered the breadbasket of Badghis. However, it was being used for poppy production by the Taliban, who had control of the area. Without control of the valley, U.S. forces determined that stability in the province would be elusive. DIB stood at the center of both the problem and the solution.

Progress was frustratingly stagnant for a year, despite offers of development projects, hiring a local police force, and establishment of essential services like medical care and education. Equally challenging, even after the head elder, Haji Hafi, professed his loyalty to the United States, there was still no progress. Perplexed by the lack of control Hafi displayed over the valley, intelligence efforts were increased to determine the drivers of instability along with more information about the cultural dimensions of the problem.

Biweekly *shuras* (council meetings) were not providing the information needed to fully understand the politics within the valley. During the shuras, there were subtle indications that certain elders were controlling information flow. Why this was happening was not apparent until additional information was gathered from the locals within DIB. An active patrolling program focused on discussions with residents within the safety of their Afghan homes. It took a year for the locals to step outside their traditional distrust of outsiders to confide in Marines, nonetheless it was a breakthrough.

Perhaps the most important information gleaned from the visits was a clearer picture of the political structures. It quickly became apparent that the political hierarchy being presented to Americans was not only extremely simplistic, but purposely skewed and inaccurate. The political structure within the village had been turned on its head by the Taliban. The self-proclaimed village elder, Haji Hafi, had come to power using the barrel of a gun and exerting his control of the valley's poppy trade. Haji Hafi's position as the leader of the valley was artificial. He wielded power through intimidation, which made him irrelevant in the eyes of the tribal elders. In effect, he had power but no real authority within the valley.

As a result, the traditional elders in the valley had been marginalized by Hafi. The elders exerted their power and authority by rising up against Hafi and providing information on his activities as a Taliban leader. Hafi was arrested and DIB began to turn around. The local shuras were now much more productive, and countless village stability programs were implemented.

Reflecting on the operation produces several lessons. First, things are not always as they seem. Haji Hafi was quick to come forward and claim absolute power in the valley. Despite having knowledge of other units making the same mistake, Marines jumped at a "friendly face." U.S. forces should have taken a more pragmatic approach to understanding cultural dimensions within the valley before taking action. Had U.S. forces taken the time to understand the local culture, the realization that a head elder could not have authority over five tribes would have been obvious. Marines complicated their work by accepting Haji Hafi's offer of cooperation, alienating the true power brokers. The year-long delay in productivity was the cost of the misunderstanding.

Another lesson learned is to use the enemy's own lack of understanding of the political structure against them. Within DIB, the Taliban had marginalized the traditional leaders. This was a tremendous missed opportunity for U.S. forces to drive a wedge between valley tribes and the Taliban. With the right questions in hand, a mistake like this can be avoided. Questioning the dynamics of the cultural dimensions is certainly a good place to start.

Gender Issues

The Dilemma of Female Detainees

Lieutenant Colonel Eric C. Dill
U.S. Marine Corps

Unbeknownst to most U.S. military personnel serving in Iraq, one of the primary grievances against the Coalition was the matter of detainees. The detention of suspected Iraqi insurgents was an incisive topic that regularly appeared in Muslim-oriented media and was the primary motivator for recruitment into the insurgency. The most intense grievance was the detention of 11 Iraqi females who had attempted suicide bombings against the Coalition. Their detention was generally unknown to Coalition members and the Western world, but was known about and abhorred across the entire *umma* (Muslim community). As pressure mounted, a solution was required to resolve the umma's grievances regarding these female detainees, without returning them to a situation where they might once again become suicide bombers. Members of the U.S. military leadership analyzed and synthesized the dimensions of social structure, political structure, and beliefs to develop a culturally appropriate solution to the female detainee situation.

The female detainees presented Coalition planners with a problem that did not reconcile with their worldview of the position and status of women, criminal punishment, and political power and authority. The United States was careful not to use the term "prisoner" when referring to people held in captivity by the Coalition. The detainees were neither convicted in a criminal court nor prisoners of war. However, the Arabic word for detainee translates to hostage. Thus, the Muslim media routinely communicated information to their audience about the status and plight of the American-held female "hostages." This was an affront to all Muslims and a dilemma for the Coalition.

Without the benefit of formal anthropological training, planners considered the roles of age, gender, class, tribal identity, ethnicity, and religion to understand what would motivate a Muslim woman to detonate a suicide rig strapped to her chest in a crowded setting.

For various violations of the social code, all 11 women had no prospect of marrying and producing children. Since marrying and having as many sons as possible is considered the purpose and duty of a Muslim woman over the age of 16 in this particular cultural group, their unmarriageable status was preeminent in the women's rationale to commit suicide. The planners concluded that the social structure and cultural beliefs regarding women's roles in Sunni Iraqi society fostered the lack of self-worth and exclusion felt by the women who had attempted to kill Coalition members by detonating a suicide vest.

The social and political structure also provided a solution for the female detainees. The destabilization of Iraq had shifted the power back to tribal leaders, who were willing to work with the Coalition to resolve the problem. Sunni Iraqi men marry up to four women and the marriages are usually arranged by the tribe. Therefore, if the "mores"[24] violated by the females could be waived by the tribe, then marriages could be arranged. The stratified tribal structure of Iraq allowed for powerful tribal leaders to direct lower level tribal leaders to absolve the females and find willing husbands for them.

Interestingly, the largest opposition to the solution was expressed by female members of the Coalition who viewed the plight of the female detainees from the lens of their worldview with regards to social structure. Arranged marriages do not coalesce with the worldview of most U.S. citizens. However, when offered this plan, the Iraqi female detainees expressed elation. This surprised and altered the opinion of some of those opposed to arranging marriages for the females.

The Coalition reconciled this issue according to the unique cultural dimensions of the Iraq/Arab/Sunni cultural group. In this case, as the planners attempted to define the problem and identify the motives of these women, they recognized that the cultural group to which these women belonged was significantly different from their own. Eventually, a solution presented itself that would have been inconceivable if the planners had been bound by the parameters of an American concept of social structure, political structure, and beliefs.

---

[24] Mores are implicit or explicit cultural rules regarding acceptable and forbidden behaviors.

Gender as an Operational Challenge and Opportunity in Military Operations

Major Misty J. Posey
U.S. Marine Corps

While deployed to Iraq during Operation Iraqi Freedom, a military police (MP) officer unwittingly created a commotion when she removed her goggles and *balaclava*—a cloth headgear that covers the whole head—exposing a feminine face and blonde hair wound into a tight bun. Until the moment she removed her head gear, the indigenous men in the area had naturally assumed that she was a male Marine. She was positioned behind a vehicle-mounted heavy machine gun and had been aggressively gesticulating orders to civilians and junior Marines. Upon realization that she was a woman, a shockwave coursed through the bewildered men in the area. The female Marine's presence in the convoy was anomalous to the cultural norms in Iraq, which prohibit women from working outside of the home, let alone serving in the military. The fact that she was manning a machine gun and providing security was even more astonishing.

News of the female Marine's presence in the local area spread quickly. Soon, the group of bystanders swelled to several times its original size and concentrated around the female Marine. Curious and incredulous men from all around—brothers, sons, uncles, cousins, and neighbors—came to view for themselves the "woman doing a man's job." Although the crowd was not blatantly hostile, the atmosphere was tense, for Iraqi men did not respond well to taking orders from a woman. The crowd grew so large and animated that the security team began to focus their efforts on trying to limit the curiosity generated by the presence and assertiveness of the female Marine, which made the MP's task of providing convoy security exceedingly difficult.

The problem with a female Marine providing security was that she was performing a task that in Iraq had been gender-coded for men. This cross-cultural issue was linked to the social structure of the Iraqi culture group and the biological characteristics of gender.[25] In Iraq, at this time, women's "everyday" participation in society did not permit working outside of the home, much less publically displaying authority and power over men.

To operate more effectively, the team leader made the female Marine less conspicuous to the local male population. She still operated outside of the firm-base with her security team, but she performed tasks that limited direct contact with gender-segregated male groups and gender-separated spaces designated for men. She also kept her face and head covered as much as practical. This helped make the team's interactions with the male populace more effective in the unit's area of operations. Conversely, her team leader made her presence conspicuous when it was prudent to do so, such as when the team came in contact with indigenous women. In this case, it was helpful to have an overt female presence to search, question, and establish rapport with this important segment of society.

Due to the tumult caused by the female Marine's violation of gender-coded social norms, the unit learned that it needed to be able to understand the social structure of the community in which it operated since a person's position in the social structure was partly determined by gender. By understanding the attitudes about gender and the appropriate roles for men and women, the Marines were able to interact more effectively with the local population and military and police forces. Practically, the unit learned that including both male and female Marines in their security teams allowed them access to critical domains that single-gender teams could not enter. The Marines learned that, outside of public view, local women exercised influential and powerful roles but that, in public, it was important for men to display authority and power.[26]

---

[25] Salmoni and Holmes-Eber, 109 and 122.
[26] Ibid., 129.

At the Checkpoint

Major Jason A. Borovies
U.S. Marine Corps

This case analyzes and discusses the resolution of a cross-cultural challenge that I personally encountered during a combat deployment to Iraq. The challenge was related to local perceptions of female search procedures at checkpoints manned by U.S. Marines along with Iraqi Security Forces. The setting was Barwanah, a small, rural town in al-Anbar Province's western Euphrates River valley. Resolution of the issue required patience, understanding, and flexibility on the part of my Marines and me.

The Marine unit that preceded ours in the area had experienced a horrific suicide attack on one of its checkpoints. The attack was conducted by a male fighter dressed as a woman to circumvent search procedures. The threat of similar, future attacks by disguised insurgents, or even women hostile to Coalition forces, drove my command to implement self-search procedures at all checkpoints. These were designed to mitigate the risk of an explosive-vest armed person closing to lethal distance with Marines and Iraqi Security Forces operating detailed search areas. In the case of women, these procedures required that they pull their *abayas* (loose, flowing robes) taught across their bodies while maintaining a safe distance from the checkpoint. This action would disclose the outline of an explosive vest or belt concealed under clothing. Although this practice provided our Marines with improved protection, it was unacceptable to the local population.

The population's negative view of female self-search procedures was linked to their belief systems. Mores[27] regarding the position of, and protections accorded to, women in Muslim society forbid objectification along with public disclosure of the female form. Local offense to our search procedures was reinforced by a syncretic[28] mixture of traditional Islamic beliefs, which had been mag-

---

[27] Mores are implicit or explicit cultural rules regarding acceptable and forbidden behaviors.
[28] Syncretism is the practice of mixing religious beliefs with local traditions and practices.

nified by the inherently conservative nature of the rural community in which we were operating. Furthermore, the masculine dominated society of Barwanah was insulted by the perceived public degradation of their women caused by self-search procedures. Friction between local belief systems and force protection concerns threatened to undermine the generally positive relationship that we enjoyed with Barwanah's people.

In the interests of maintaining a harmonious relationship with the local population and ensuring that the environment remained sympathetic to Coalition forces, we decided to modify female search procedures so that they would be less objectionable. We constructed a three-sided chamber at each of our checkpoints into which a woman could step to perform a self-search. These chambers were situated such that only a female Marine would have a direct line of sight into the chamber. This guaranteed that local women would be accorded some degree of privacy, even when conducting the self-searches necessitated by force protection concerns. Furthermore, we demonstrated these new search procedures to local tribal, government, and security force leaders at each of the checkpoints. In so doing, we effectively allayed the local population's concerns, yet were able to continue providing our Marines and partnered Iraqi personnel with the required level of protection.

In conclusion, the belief systems of Barwanah's population led to a cross-cultural challenge associated with female search procedures at checkpoints. Mores and a syncretism of Islamic beliefs combined with conservative rural attitudes created tension. Recognition of this tension, willingness to compromise, and involvement of local leadership in the resolution process enabled my Marines and me to overcome the challenge.

Assessment

Culture and Evaluation
of Methods of Assessment

Major Corey J. Frederickson
Princess Patricia's Canadian Light Infantry

When military forces operate in foreign countries, the inevitable clash of cultures can have a major impact on the success or failure of military operations, particularly when conducting counterinsurgency (COIN) or stability operations where the focus is (or at least should be) on the population. People of different cultures may react differently in the same circumstances, and a lack of understanding of this fact can lead to the undermining of the military effort. For example, the assessment of measures of effectiveness (MoE) is very important in the COIN fight. There are the observations of the tangibles—number of attacks on military and civilian targets, whether the market is open or not, people demonstrating in the streets, etcetera. However, the intangibles perhaps matter more—for example, the perceptions of the population. This essay will discuss the difficulty my unit faced in assessing the perceptions of a foreign civilian population and how we eventually resolved the situation—at least to some satisfaction.

In 2008, while employed in the Canadian Task Force Afghanistan, I and a small number of Canadian and Afghan soldiers deployed to Maywand District, Kandahar Province, in what was to be the first permanent Coalition presence in the area to date.[29] After a couple months of operations, we wished to implement some MoE to give us an azimuth check regarding our strategy. We canvassed the local population, asking such questions as: "Do you feel secure? Are you happy with the government? Do you trust the coalition and the Afghan security forces?" Inevitably, the responses were overwhelmingly positive; one would think that we were hugely successful—undoubtedly unrealistically so.

What we did not understand was that there were social norms,

---

[29] Personal experience of the author.

part of the cultural dimension of belief systems, at play when the local population was answering our questions.[30] It was eventually explained to us by our Afghan security force partners that, when locals are engaged in conversation with people in positions of authority, the most likely responses are generally very positive in nature. Essentially, they were saying that most Afghans simply tell you what they think you want to hear. They do this primarily because they want to give the impression of being a "good" citizen and, secondly, because they do not want to cause trouble for themselves by appearing to be critical of the authorities. From a Western perspective, our questions were designed to elicit direct and honest responses, regardless of whether these responses may have been an indictment of our efforts. Our failure to understand this social norm (also, perhaps, the Afghans' inability to understand our true motives in asking the questions) led to an inaccurate evaluation of the population's true perception of their environment, something that eventually became clear to us through the actions of the population as well as the insurgents.

Eventually, we learned that the problem was not the questions we were asking but rather the manner in which we asked them. By offering a list of issues and asking the local population to prioritize the most important concerns that the government should address, we were able to ascertain a more accurate picture of their perceptions. Instead of asking, "Do you feel secure?" or "Is the government doing a good job?" we said, "Please prioritize where the government should focus its efforts: security, building schools, the economy, or eliminating corruption." By changing the structure of the question, we were able to get the answers we were looking for, while still respecting the social norms of the population.

This is only one small example of how the understanding of culture is an important part of military operations. If we had a better understanding of the Afghan culture before deploying we might have avoided the ineffective assessments. As it was, we eventually learned—as did our follow-on rotations—from our mistakes.

---

[30] Salmoni and Holmes-Eber, 205.

Part III:

**Cultural Challenges
in the Joint Operating Environment**

Security Cooperation and
Advisor Training

Mirror Imaging the Afghan Local Police: Environmental Considerations for Developing Indigenous Police Forces

Major Ryan D. Shea
U.S. Marine Corps

While serving in Afghanistan from the summer of 2010 to the spring of 2011, Special Operations Task Force–West encountered numerous cross-cultural challenges that affected our ability to conduct operations in the Regional Command–West (RC-W) area of operations. One operational concept in particular, the Afghan Local Police (ALP) program, demanded a high level of cultural awareness to ensure its success. Throughout initial planning and early execution of the ALP program, our lack of focus on the physical environment of the Afghan culture, specifically the means and patterns of transportation and communication, resulted in an ineffective allocation of resources that ultimately hindered the expansion of the program.

The development of the ALP concept and the subsequent implementation of the program took place during our deployment. Raising a new indigenous police force from the numerous villages spread throughout rural RC-W was immensely challenging. However, once these forces were on hand, training and equipping them proved even more difficult. Without the foresight to consider the Afghan culture, our planning team "mirror-imaged" and developed an equipment set we thought we would need if we were in the ALP's position.

Because the primary mission of the ALP was to patrol and respond to incidents in their respective villages, we equipped the ALP with pickup trucks to facilitate mobility. Once these trucks were in possession of the ALP, it did not take long for us to realize that we failed somewhere in the planning process. Accidents, poor maintenance, cannibalization, running out of gas, and an inability to patrol and respond to incidents were all common occurrences that plagued our ability to get the ALP program operational. By mirror imaging and equipping the ALP with pickup trucks and communication suites similar to the equipment we had, we failed to consider how the rural

Afghan culture uses the environment for transportation and communication.

Villagers in the rural areas of RC-W live off the land adjacent to their village and rarely leave the area. Meager unimproved roads, dirt tracks, and narrow mountain passes connect one village to another. Without a requirement to travel long distances, villagers travel by foot and animal. These villages have very narrow "road" networks that weave between mud-walled compounds that typically house multiple families. This compactness creates intimacy that enables word-of-mouth communications, strong local relationships, and trust among neighbors.

In planning, we failed to consider that the modes and patterns of transportation and communication in a typical RC-W village do not require the infrastructure that we as Americans often take for granted. Without paved roads, gas stations, and vehicle repair shops, pickup trucks are useless. Patrolling and rapidly responding to emergencies by truck is impossible down the narrow "roads" of these villages. Communication suites are impractical when the locals communicate by word-of-mouth. By not considering the physical environment of Afghan culture, we provided the ALP with equipment that was useless and in some cases harmful.

Our task force learned from these mistakes. Specifically, we understood that we had to consider the forms of transportation, support services and materials, and infrastructure used by the Afghan villagers to ensure the success of the ALP program. Taking these principles of operational culture into consideration, we took the vehicles away from the ALP and developed the neighborhood headquarters concept. This concept involved assisting the ALP in developing small bases of operation spread throughout their villages in such a way as to allow them to patrol and respond to incidents on foot. These neighborhood headquarters also embraced word-of-mouth communication by providing a place for locals to seek assistance from someone they know and trust. By integrating cultural considerations into the planning process for the remainder of our deployment, our task force ensured the sustainability of the ALP program.

Working with the Iraqi Police in ar-Ramadi, Iraq

Major Marcus J. Mainz
U.S. Marine Corps

During the height of the al-Anbar Awakening in 2007, I was the Lima Company Commander 2/7 in ar-Ramadi, Iraq. A seemingly simple problem arose in our area as the battalion was attempting to transition the vehicle checkpoints to the Iraqis. The battalion had spent man-hours and thousands of dollars planning and building a checkpoint on the major highway through the heart of the city. Unfortunately, the battalion could not get the Iraqi police to operate the checkpoint. No amount of higher-level meetings with the chief of police or mayor seemed to be working. Day after day, the checkpoint remained unmanned and the battalion was convinced that they needed to fire the current local police chief.

The problem was not that the local police chief was ineffective or that the Iraqi police officers were lazy. Rather, the real issue was our lack of understanding of their social and political structures. American forces assumed the police structure would function similar to ours, and that giving an order at the top of the organizational chart was going to affect action at the bottom. I discovered this was not the case when I was given the responsibility to solve the problem.

My relationship with the locals was different from the battalion because I lived in the city with Iraqis. The average ratio of Marine to Iraqi on my six bases was 1 to 13. During my four months of living in the city, the sheiks, imams, locals, and interpreters assisted me in learning the best methods of effectiveness in ar-Ramadi.

Seeking to solve the problem, I requested to have dinner with the local sheik and all of the local police chiefs in my area of responsibility. All six of the local police chiefs were of the same tribe and five of them were cousins. Apparently, months before our arrival, the local tribesmen had made the decision to rise up against the insurgency. As a result, the tribesmen were commissioned as the local police force. Their structure at the lowest levels resembled more of their tribal structure than it did an actual police organization.

After two hours of eating, smoking, and drinking tea, I told the sheik that I had a problem and that I needed his help. I mentioned that I had lost much face with my current boss and that I was going to be fired because the checkpoint was unmanned. The sheik and police enlightened me that the checkpoint was merely a distraction and the insurgents would never try to come through it. They explained that no amount of cajoling or threatening the formal power structure was going to make the tribesmen operate a checkpoint they did not deem as essential.

Instead, the police were currently using their best men to set up random checkpoints around the city where the enemy would surely be trying to infiltrate. Before the Awakening, this tribe had earned a living by smuggling. They were employing that prior knowledge to catch the insurgents with techniques that had stopped them previously. The sheik and police laid out for me their ingenious and invisible plans that had been preventing the insurgents from coming back to ar-Ramadi. At the end of the meeting, the sheik patted me on the back and said "Don't worry. You are part of our tribe now and you will not be fired. I will fix your problem." That next morning, the checkpoint was manned and remained so until I left three months later. By understanding their social and political structure, we were able satisfy and empower everyone while accomplishing our military and political objectives.

Redesigning an Afghan District's Security Plan

Major John C. Gianopoulos
U.S. Marine Corps

In March 2011, nearly all of the Afghan National Army (ANA) battalions stationed in Afghanistan's Musa Qala District were positioned inside the relative safety of the outer shell of the district security "bubble." The units manning the dangerous outer shell of the bubble were U.S. Marine and Afghan National Police (ANP) units. This arrangement of security forces was detrimental to every organization and hindered progress toward transition of security responsibilities from U.S. Marines to Afghan Forces. Changing the security arrangement was crucial, but implementing change proved far harder than American leaders expected.

The district's U.S. Marine commander aimed to redesign the district's security system to ripen the area for transition while improving the abilities of the Afghan security organizations. The Marine commander's goal was to get the ANA commander to move his companies to the outer shell of the security bubble and for the ANP commander to move his units to the interior of the bubble—areas of the district that were safer and ready for policing.

The Afghan security and political organizations in Musa Qala were quite resistant to a major change in the division of security labor. It was not until U.S. Marine leaders and Afghan officials understood and addressed certain aspects of the social and political dimensions of Afghan culture at work in relationships in Musa Qala that these American and Afghan leaders could realize the goal of rearranging the security forces in the district.

Musa Qala's political structure was comprised of several formal leaders, including the U.S. Marine battalion commander, the district governor (DG), the district chief of police (DCOP), and the ANA battalion commander (ANA CO). However, there was no clear hierarchy among the organizations. Thus, no leader could direct another. On the other hand, the social dimension of the relationship between these formal political leaders was characterized by an unequal status between the between the ANA and ANP commanders and their organizations and by complications arising from ethnic differences between the local, Pashtun Afghan National Police, and the foreign, mostly-Tajik or Hazara Afghan National Army. Due to the lack of unified command and the problematic interrelationships, the Marine commander realized that there would have to be negotiation and mutual agreement to execute the plan to redesign the district security system.

The Marine commander decided that the key to group consensus was to convince the DCOP of the merits of the new security plan. The DCOP doubled as a powerful informal leader in Musa Qala. He was a local man famous for his bravery and leadership in fighting both the Soviets and the Taliban, who enjoyed a reputation as an effective police commander and all-round authority figure in the district. As the Marine commander influenced the DCOP to accept the Marine view, the DCOP began to directly influence the district governor on the viability of the Marine plan and to indirectly pressure and shame the ANA CO to acquiesce to the Marine plan.

Over several days in July 2011, the ANA and ANP effectively switched positions in the district security scheme; the ANP moved to the interior and the ANA moved to the exterior of the perimeter. The switch improved the security situation, readied the district for transition, and all organizations benefitted. The ANP became more connected to their communities and improved their skills. The move strengthened the ANA battalion, and the ANA's status was boosted in the eyes of the population and the district leadership. The DG was made to look wiser and the Marines on the outer shell got a more capable partner—the ANA battalion.

In the spring, the Marines thought that the issue of redesigning the district security plan would be a simple matter of showing the Afghan leaders that the new plan made sense and that the Afghans would adopt it. Yet, in the end, the move was only made possible by the Marine commander and other leaders seeing the complexity of the social and political dimensions of the stakeholders' relationships and finding ways to subtly influence formal leaders to accept and effect change.

Permission to Coordinate:
There Must Be Homage to Authority
in Ecuador 2009–10

Major August R. Immel
U.S. Marine Corps

The mission of Security Cooperation Offices (SCOs) located in U.S. Embassies in countries around the globe is simply to assist the development of a partner country's security forces by arranging the training, equipping, and advising of those forces. Such a mission requires continuous interaction with foreign counterparts to develop priorities for military assistance programs designed to improve a shortfall in the preparedness or proficiency of the foreign military. In each and every case, the official approval for a program's implementation must be given by designated political authorities. From 2009 to 2010 in Ecuador, the level of that designated political office holding approval authority transitioned from an individual service chief to the *Comando Conjunto* (Ecuadorian Joint Chiefs of Staff) and finally to the Minister of Defense (MoD). This shift, which corresponded to changes in the Ecuadorian political structure, ultimately stifled effective security cooperation efforts between the Ecuadorian and U.S. military at the time.

In the summer of 2010, per an official memorandum from the office of the MoD, even a meeting between an officer of the U.S. Military Group (USMILGP, or the title of the SCO in Ecuador) and a mid-level officer in one of the armed services required MoD approval. All military-to-military contact now required the approval of the highest civil authority directing the armed forces of Ecuador short of the president himself. This notable bureaucratic obstacle created by the Ecuadorian political authority was designed to limit unsanctioned interaction between U.S. and Ecuadorian military officers. Much more importantly, however, this increase in the level of approval authority was a power demonstration by the Ecuadorian president.

The president of Ecuador in 2009-10 was outspokenly anti-American and observably afraid of any contestation for authority. With increased military assistance from the United States as a result of anti-drug funding, the Ecuadorian president perceived a potential growth in the power of the military through its collaboration with the United States. Along with many South American countries, Ecuador experienced a number of coups, including the most recent in 2000. Fearful of any military attempt to remove him from office, the president of Ecuador began to tighten his authority over the military.

This relationship between civil and military authorities demonstrated a problem within the political structure of Ecuador: the president held legitimate authority but was fearful of losing his means to exercise power.[31] As a result of the general distrust of the military, the president, through the MoD, forced all U.S.-Ecuadorian military interaction to be approved at the highest civilian levels, apparently attempting to limit the growth of the power of the military. To continue receiving military assistance from the United States, members of the Ecuadorian military were now forced to recognize the authority of the president and adhere to the stipulations of the official memorandum.

The obedience to the memorandum's requirements resulted in a communication process between militaries that took up to three weeks to simply schedule a meeting. The president's perception of a potential power struggle resulted in increased difficulty for the US-MILGP to provide assistance to and ultimately limited the development of the Ecuadorian military. The USMILGP saw a decline in interactions and military programs as a result of the increased bureaucracy.

With an understanding of the operational culture in Ecuador, an important lesson can be incorporated by the USMILGP for future military interactions. The existing political structure of the country will have a tremendous impact on the amount and type of military programs allowed to take place. Recognizing this fact and understanding the effects of the existing political structure will allow increased efficiency in the delivery of training, equipment, and advice through the establishment of realistic expectations based on what the civil authorities will approve. Knowing the political structure in advance can help to prepare appropriate timelines, military program proposals, and funding criteria designed with a better chance of gaining approval.

---

[31] Salmoni and Homes-Eber, 154.

Joint Operations

Coordination in a Multinational Flight Training Exercise

Lieutenant Colonel Derek M. Brannon
U.S. Marine Corps

Multinational aviation training exercises are commonplace within the Pacific Command's area of operation and assist in the development of tactics, techniques, and procedures for future integration of partner forces in operational plans. Integral to each of the training exercises are debriefs attended by all of the participants, including opposing forces (OPFOR) and air intercept controllers. During a group debrief for an exercise training flight, a young U.S. flight leader questioned the validity of one of the Thai aviator's simulated missile shots that had resulted in a failed mission for the U.S. flight. In reply to the inquiry, another Thai aviator responded with a suitable answer, to the dismay of the U.S. flight leader. The U.S. flight leader pressed for a direct answer from the original Thai aviator without receiving a response. Suddenly, after several inquiries, the entire Thai flight formation stood up and walked out of the group debrief. The incident had compounding repercussions to training, which would not be solved prior to the completion of the exercise.

Aspects from three operational culture dimensions had an influence on the incident. The first dimension to be discussed is social structure and the influence of position. Of note, position and rank in both the Thai Air Force and the U.S. military have a similar influence on good conduct and discipline in their respective forces. In the above incident, the U.S. aviator was a captain with limited experience on his first deployment. In contrast, the primary Thai aviator was an experienced colonel who was providing instruction to his flight leader, a captain. A second aspect of position that should be analyzed is the issue of status. The status of the Thai colonel in the flight during the training evolution was that of a wingman. In U.S. procedures, a wingman is always subservient to the flight leader regardless of rank. Since the Thai captain was the flight leader, from the U.S. perspective, he was responsible for the overall conduct of the flight and the primary debrief communicator. The U.S. perspective or belief system regarding status, rank, and appropriate interaction, however, was quite different from that of the Thai formation.

From an American perspective, the issue of disrespect due to a difference in rank would not seem to be a causal factor in the Thai formation's departure from the debrief since the U.S. aviator was respectful throughout the incident. In the U.S. military belief system, a lower-ranking officer can provide critique to a senior officer in the appropriate setting as long as the comments are factually based. However, in Thai culture, the belief in "face" or public honor plays an important role in person-to-person interactions. In this case, the younger U.S. captain's persistent questioning and critique of a more senior Thai colonel, no matter how factually based, was likely viewed as humiliating, resulting in a public loss of face.

Although the Thai colonel was only a wingman, in a public display of his authoritative status, he walked out of the debrief and affected the entire evolution. Interestingly, in a display of unity, the remainder of the Thai flight followed the colonel out of the debrief without any hesitation. Hence, the final cultural dimension, pertaining to the incident, would be political structure and the authority and power that the colonel held in the group. The incident is unique in the fact that approximately 50 aviators from five different countries and Services were attending the debrief and witnessed the incident.

In retrospect, the departure of just the Thai colonel would have had little effect on the training evolution. Yet, the departure of the remaining Thai contingent immediately ended the evolution. The prestige and skill of the Thai colonel supported his display of power based on not only his formal rank but also his informal influence on the other Thai aviators. Therefore, the link between the social and political dimensions in this incident cannot be separated.

In conclusion, predeployment training should include information on basic rank structures and positions, but also awareness of the unintended consequences that interactions may have on cultural relationships. In this incident, the exercise continued as planned but the U.S. captain was unable to lead another flight at the request of the Thai leadership. Additionally, the U.S. captain was unable to attain flight leadership upgrades and the squadron failed to complete several of its training goals for the exercise. The influence of the Thai colonel, in conjunction with the public support from the other Thai aviators, was a notable example of their operational culture. As a result of the repercussions of this event, subsequent U.S. predeployment training includes briefs on these aspects of Thai culture.

Coalition Compromise in a No-Fly Zone Over Libya

Major Steven Leutner
U.S. Air Force

In 2011, the world watched as Muammar Gaddafi engaged in a brutal crackdown on the Libyan population that, as part of the "Arab Spring," was rising up against his regime. The United Nations and NATO acted and began to implement a no-fly zone over Libya. Not all countries, however, supported the no-fly zone, and there was growing concern that the NATO action could be construed by the Arab world as another example of a Western Coalition invading and implementing regime change. A political solution was needed and quickly. An Arab country needed to join the Coalition to increase the legitimacy of NATO operations. This decision posed both cross-cultural challenges and opportunities that had to be worked through at all levels of war.

At the time, there was considerable acrimony to countries in the West and revolutionary currents ran through the Arab streets. To prevent the perception of another Western invasion, it became critical to find a willing Arab ally that would join the NATO Coalition to enforce the UN mandate. Fortunately, Jordan with its close Western ties was willing to sign up, and soon thereafter several Royal Jordanian Air Force (RJAF) F-16s deployed to support NATO operations.

While the political legitimacy solution had been solved, the solution created a host of challenges at lower levels. First, the physical environment was vastly different for the RJAF. Their doctrine has always centered on defending their country and projecting power from their home bases, not expeditionary Coalition warfighting. They were able to acclimatize to the radically different environmental setting as Coalition partner air forces allowed RJAF maintenance personnel access to maintenance facilities and RJAF pilots were able to align their operational planning and communications systems with NATO F-16 squadrons.

The next challenge was partly a result of the previously mentioned doctrine and also the Jordanian economy. Jordan is a poor country with limited resources (it does not have significant oil deposits) and large segments of their population subsist on an agriculturally and pastorally based economy. As a result, the government cannot fund their military well and, in the case of the RJAF F-16s, they were only capable of basic air defense missions and dropping "dumb" bombs. The risks of collateral damage were too great to allow dumb bomb employment. Since the Coalition did not anticipate a notable air threat from Libya, the decision was made that the Jordanian contribution would be to defend the Coalition against all Libyan fighters. The Jordanians happily accepted their role, as they were the only ones given the "honor" of being solely dedicated to protecting the Coalition from air attack.

The final challenge was tactical—their pilots were not trained to the same standard as other air forces. In the Jordanian Air Force, their leadership structure is based on hereditary, political connections, and age. By contrast, in most NATO countries, fighter communities are meritocracies. Many of the senior RJAF pilots were not proficient. While they could take off, fly a one-hour sortie, and then land from a base just fine, more complex tasks such as rendezvousing with an air tanker, flying a six-hour missions, flying with hundreds of other aircraft, and speaking the international language of aviation (English) was very challenging for them. Once again, a solution was needed. NATO invited the RJAF to join the formation of a Coalition country also flying F-16s. They made sure to allow the RJAF to save face by agreeing to always have highly experienced pilots lead the formation, and the new procedures were done under the auspices that it was easier for air traffic controllers to manage one large formation as opposed to multiple smaller ones.

Two key lessons can be learned from this experience. First, one must be aware of culture at all levels of an operation and understand that, while it may place some restrictions on an operation, cultural issues are much easier dealt with in advance. Second, communication and understanding are key. NATO could not have come up with these solutions without open communication with the RJAF. In this regard, NATO benefitted from their existing knowledge of the RJAF, gleaned from an air exercise that the Jordanians had hosted during the previous year. The cultural and operational lessons learned during this previous partnership thus served as a solid foundation for building a successful coalition during the Libyan operation.

Regional Air and Missile Defense in the Western Pacific: Overcoming Cross-Cultural Differences

Lieutenant Commander Adam D. Wieder
U.S. Navy

Prior to the "pivot" to the Pacific in the fall of 2011, I served as an integrated air and missile defense (IAMD) planner on the head-quarters staff of the U.S. 7th Fleet. IAMD in the Western Pacific presents unique challenges with the conventional threats of the People's Republic of China and the Democratic People's Republic of Korea (i.e., North Korea), both of which boast significant ballistic missile capability within range of regional allies, partners, and U.S. bases. Planning and execution in this environment requires joint and combined solutions that incorporate the IAMD capabilities of the United States, Japan, and the Republic of Korea (ROK). How-ever, there are many deep-seated social, political, and physical di-mensions that present challenges to coalition building. Planners, operators, and commanders within the U.S. Pacific Command must pursue the resolution of cross-cultural challenges as they integrate U.S. and Japanese IAMD capabilities in the larger joint and com-bined warfighting architecture.

Linking this problem to dimensions of Japanese operational cul-ture, three particular examples come to mind. First, the primacy of Japanese homeland intertwines the physical, social, and political aspects of their culture. Second, internal physical and social di-mensions affect Japanese international relations with the United States. Finally, historical, regional, and social dimensions cloud present-day international relations.

Defending the integrity and sovereignty of Japanese territory ranks first in priority of considerations. For Japanese self-defense forces, failure is not an option. Socially, the historic Samurai Bushido code influences this belief. Relating to IAMD planning and execution, this near-religious belief manifests itself in a politically and socially driven defense design that values centers of cultural significance over military or governmental necessity. Operationally, this may lead to inefficient use of defending assets and insufficient coverage over more critical military infrastructure. Additionally, the Japanese constitution's prohibition of offensive military forces complicates this problem by restricting military commanders from potential mission options that would gain defensive efficiencies by placing forces in an offensive posture.

Japanese internal politics must accommodate multiple internal cultural differences, which in turn weigh on international relations. Nowhere is this more evident than in Okinawa, where the basing of U.S. Marines stresses an already contentious cultural rift between the native Okinawans and the central Japanese government. Okinawan people see themselves as a unique ethnic group separate from the Japanese. Therefore the resolution of U.S. basing on Okinawa often plays an important role in both national politics and international diplomacy. This situation hinders IAMD planning and execution when considering force size and available basing for joint and combined forces in Japan.

Regional history, namely the political and social aspects of Imperial Japanese domination in the Western Pacific, presents a challenge to present-day international relations for Japan. Centuries of resentment and distrust fostered by regional historic events that extend even to the conflicts of the mid-to-late twentieth century, resonate in current relations between Japan and the ROK. This cultural memory does not have uniform effects across the respective populations. While the practical nature of military-to-military relations allows the defense establishments to overlook these issues, the politicians either cannot or will not overlook the same. In the realm of IAMD, this residual resentment creates strife in developing the formal agreements for information sharing, among other aspects. In a warfighting discipline that requires seamless command-and-control (C2) networks for swift decision making on composite information, U.S. forces may be the only Coalition partner with the complete picture. Often C2 architectures are fractured purposely so that neither Japanese nor Korean information can be seen by the other.

The challenges described above were not resolved during my

tenure at U.S. 7th Fleet. In fact, in the near future, the greater emphasis placed on the Pacific may further highlight some of these cultural dimensions and the operational challenges they pose. Nonetheless, U.S. and Japanese Forces have made great operational strides in cooperation and coordination. Continued progress will depend on planners, operators, and commanders that understand the physical, social, and political dimensions of the Japanese operational culture, and thereby address coordination points in terms that accommodate the Japanese perspective on their homeland and regional standing. Ultimately, as the United States looks ahead, answering the growing North Korean threat and rising power of China will require a Coalition of regional nations that uses cross-cultural differences to strengthen rather than hinder the alliance.

References

Fraser, A. W. and N. Rose. "A Short Guide to Training Indigenous Soldiers in the North-West Mobile Force (NORFORCE)." Unofficial Australian Army Unit Publication, Darwin, NT: November 2000.

Holmes-Eber, P., P. M. Scanlon, and A. L. Hamlen, eds. *Applications in Operational Culture*: Perspectives from the Field. Quantico, VA: Marine Corps University Press, 2009.

Horton, D. (ed). *The Encyclopedia of Aboriginal Australia*: *Aboriginal and Torres Strait Islander History, Society and Culture*. Darwin, NT: Australian Institute of Aboriginal and Torres Strait Islander Studies, Aboriginal Studies Press, 1994.

Salmoni, B. and P. Holmes-Eber. *Operational Culture for the Warfighter*. Quantico, VA: Marine Corps University Press, 2011.

Vane, A. *North Australia Observer Unit–Unit History of an Army Surveillance Regiment*, Riverwood, NSW: Australian Military History Publications, 2000.

www.ingramcontent.com/pod-product-compliance
Lightning Source LLC
Chambersburg PA
CBHW081420270326
41931CB00015B/3344